Astral Projection

&

Astrology

The Complete Beginners Guide to Zodiac Signs, How to Travel out Of Your Body On The Astral Plane, Find True Love, Your Perfect Career And Your Personality Profile

Written By

Mia Rose

©Copyright 2019 by Mia Rose - All rights reserved.

Mia Rose

Content

Astrology

The complete guide to the Zodiac

Signs find true Love, your Perfect

Career & your Personality Profile

Written By

Mia Rose

Introduction

I want to thank you and congratulate you for getting the book, "The Complete Guide to the Signs of the Zodiac".

This book contains information on each of the traditional Western signs of the Zodiac. In a full, new, examination of the traditional Zodiac, this book looks at the popular interpretations of the signs and symbols it contains. The book also places them in context with their ancient meanings. While some astrological signs are easy to interpret, others have deeper meanings and associations now overlooked in the modern world. In this book, we explore the symbolism, both ancient and modern, as it applies to each of the signs. This book is a journey through the fascinating human traits that the Zodiac provides a reference for and, like all exciting journeys, may contain a few surprises. Also containing an introduction examining why the sky (and what was going on up there) was so important to our ancestors, this book takes a deeper look at how the influence of the stars can fashion those of us who live our lives in their shadows.

Thanks again for reading this book, I hope you enjoy it!

Reading the Sky; An Ancient View of the World

Astrology has been practiced in one form or another since at least the 2nd millennium BCE. Early Mesopotamian rulers are known to have used astrologers to define the correct time for various actions – from wars to marriages. In fact, for much of its history, the study and practice of astrology has played a significant social and political role, alongside other scientific disciplines including meteorology and medicine. Only since the 17th and 18th centuries has it declined in popularity and been replaced by astronomy as the scientific expression of the study of the heavens. This is not to say that astrology has been complete discounted by those in high places. In the 1980s Nancy Regan - the US First Lady - hired a secret, but official, White House Astrologer.

It's perhaps no surprise that from our earliest days humanity has looked to the heavens for guidance, inspiration and answers. Early humans depended, quite literally, on what the sky threw at them in terms of weather, light and seasons. It was clear that the sun, for example, had a distinct influence on what would grow and when. It was also clear that the sun did not always appear in the same positions in the sky at different times of the year, which in turn affected plants, animals and human activities on earth. It was hardly rocket science (which came much later) for ancient societies to make this connection. More advanced connections were soon made by those nations and civilizations that began to take to the seas; tides and the moon where inextricably linked, that much was clear, but how the actual mechanism worked took longer for scientists to establish.

As people began to live in cities for the first time they also began to study the world around them (and above them) more completely. With sophisticated agricultural systems came the chance for part of society to develop new areas of study. It's not a surprise then that one of the priorities for early civilizations in Mesopotamia was to understand the influence that the heavenly bodies had down on earth. The heavens were considered the homes of the gods and with the celestial bodies clearly able to control and manipulate the elements themselves (something largely beyond humanity even today) this study became a crucial part of understanding the world. The influence of the stars, the planets and the sun and moon on the earth were gradually defined and the first astrological systems and zodiacs came into being.

The Modern Zodiac

The modern Zodiac familiar in the West is based on the ancient Greek system of astrology. In turn, some elements of that earliest Mesopotamian are believed to be incorporated into the Greek Zodiac. While Eastern astrology seems to have developed along different lines, the early Greek astrological studies seem to have also heavily influenced the subject in India, and Hindu traditions have some similarities to modern Western astrology as a result.

Astrological Charts

The basic principle that is used to create an astrological chart is complex. The whole zodiac is used to establish the nature of a person's character, their potential and likely future events in their lives. Using the time, date and location of their birth, the position of each planet, and the sun and moon within the Tropical Zodiac and also their positions in relation to each other is used to create a complex 'life-path' and character assessment. This type of chart is not only complex but contains extreme detail and can be very useful for you to understand the path of your life, the challenges you may face and the opportunities that you should take (and when). However, much modern simple astrology is based simply on Sun Sign astrology – looking at the way in which your personality and life is likely to be influenced by position of the sun at your birth. The sun, so influential on the real physical world, is the signifier of your outer personality and potential and, as a starting point, in astrology this is a sensible place to begin.

Mia Rose

In this book we'll look in detail at each of the sun signs – how they influence personality, the types of career that those with each sun sign will excel in, their impact on relationships and on dealing with life's challenges. We look at one sign per chapter and will examine the profile of those that fall under the sign, good career fits, compatibilities in the romantic areas of life, traits associated with the sign and their strengths and weaknesses. You can use this book to understand the sign that you and your closest friends and associates were born with and also, should you choose to have a full horoscope created by a professional astrologer, you'll be able to use this book to understand the way in which different parts of your personality are influenced by each sign of the Zodiac.

Zodiac Controversies (the thirteenth sign).

In this book we look at the traditional and accepted version of the Zodiac. The constellations described were originally defined several thousand years ago and due to the way in which the planets (and the earth itself) 'drift' over time, there have been some changes to which constellations touch the elliptic of the Tropics. In fact the constellations have never spent equal amounts of time on this elliptic, with Virgo spending five times longer than Scorpio in the transit of the sun. The original Zodiac was an 'extrapolation' of each sign, used to split the sun signs into twelve equal length periods. The constellation of Ophiuchus, which due to the gradual drift of the earth's position, now enters the elliptic, was always recognized with the cosmology of ancient civilizations but was never considered a Zodiac sign. However, astrologers argue that the "real" positions and timings of the Zodiac have always been an interpretation and, for this reason, discount the arrival of an 'extra' sign in the Zodiac. In this book we have taken the same approach and remained true to the traditional (but fascinating) twelve signs of the Zodiac.

Mia Rose

Aries, the Ram. Leaping before Looking?

21st March – 19th April

The first sign of the zodiac Aries epitomizes youthfulness, enthusiasm and energy. This particular Ram is a Spring Ram, bursting with new energy and life. Ariens are not only the first sign of the zodiac but see themselves very much as the first in many senses of the word. Forging ahead, leading the pack and generally demanding everybody else's attention.

It's no coincidence that the zodiac symbol for Aries is highly suggestive of a new, spring shoot as well as the face and horns of a ram. Those born under this sign are initiators; they start things off. If you need a kick-start for any project the best person to call is undoubtedly an Aries. There's a downside to this; an Aries' energy is extremely forceful and focused. They love bashing their way through problems, forging ahead and leading the pack. However, they're not so good at staying with a project and seeing it through in all the boring detail. That sort of stuff, as far as your average Aries is concerned, is for the rest of us!

All that energy makes for an impulsive character and one that is quick to flare up in anger when crossed. However, Aries characters may lose their temper quickly but it subsides just as quickly as well, like a spring storm. With the outburst over, they'll be sunny, smiling and mischievous again. This can be a hard characteristic for others to get to grips with but the sheer, beguiling enthusiasm of Aries makes them easy to forgive and they'll rarely hold a grudge.

Aries people are trail blazers and they're also ruled by the planet Mars. Mars, in Roman mythology, is also the god of war. In terms of people born with the Sun in Aries this doesn't necessarily mean they're constantly fighting; it more often manifests as a fearlessness in life. They are bold, fearless and have as much courage in life as you could hope for. Once challenged (in any area of life) a person ruled by this sign will head into battle without fear or favor and almost certainly win. Aries people can make great campaigners – even for seemingly lost causes!

Aries is a fire sign – in this case think of burning desire; they're passionate in love and life. Their desire to win is strong and they work and play hard. Sport is often a serious passion for those born under this sign and is a good way to burn off all that surplus energy that is innate to those born under the sign of the Ram. In the case of Aries, the fire that burns within them is rarely destructive but is a energetic force for change, clearing obstacles and creating room for growth and success.

Aries is one of the four cardinal signs of the Zodiac. The cardinal signs all have a strong focus on change and initiating that change. Aries is possibly the strongest of all of these and is frequently seen as the pioneer of the Zodiac. Life with Aries can be fast-paced and non-stop but it's always exciting and rarely boring!

Sheepish Lovers?

Anything but, in fact. Aries are passionate and enthusiastic in all areas of life and that holds true for romance. If a person born under this sign falls for you, you won't be left wondering if they're attracted to you. They'll rush in head first and make their intentions clear. Often showering you with gifts and arranging sudden, spontaneous trips and treats. Aries people do, however, become bored very quickly. This can be challenging when trying to establish a longer term relationship with an Aries individual. They are a very independent type and need plenty of freedom in life; trying to tie an Aries down to a quiet, gently paced domestic life is likely to have them bounding off for the hills in no time. Those born under the signs of Leo and Sagittarius, both fire signs like Aries, are often well suited to this lifestyle. They have similar passions and are also strong and independent enough to balance well with the enthusiastic, energetic and fiery Aries. Those who enjoy activity, change and challenge in life will make perfect partners for Aries people, helping to keep them interested, motivated and enthusiastic in turn.

Careers – Following the Flock or Leading the Pack?

Independence is a keyword in the Arien philosophy, so working for themselves is often an ideal solution for the Aries personality. The make good leaders but will need a team of people capable of following and concentrating on details (which they can become bored with).

Sports careers suit Aries people well. They have the drive, the energy and enthusiasm to take on serious physical challenges and this type of career is possibly the ideal for many born under this sign. Aries like to win, so it's likely they'll make great sporting heroes and heroines.

Careers in sales are also a good choice. Although often forceful, Aries individuals are good negotiators – in that they'll negotiate until they've got their way! This also makes them excellent politicians and even diplomats (as long as they control that hot-hotheadedness).

Journalism, especially war correspondent, is often a good choice of career for an Aries. They will appreciate the challenge, the danger and constant movement required in this setting. Given that they are forceful at championing a cause, they can also be the perfect reporter to take the risks necessary to bring the full picture to life.

On the same theme, working for charities, NGOs or international groups in far-flung and dangerous parts of the world often suits the Aries need for challenge, danger and their ability to commit to a cause that they believe worthwhile. Ultimately, Aries will get things done, whatever it takes and they're brilliant people to have on your side!

Taurus, the Bull. The Stubborn Sensualist?

April 20th – May 20th

Bullish, stubborn, intractable? These are the sort of words you might think are associated with those born under the sign of the Bull. However, Taureans are a more complex bunch and in order to understand this complexity it's worth looking at the ruler of the sign; Venus. Venus was the Greek Goddess of Love, pleasure and beauty. Sensuality and enjoyment of the fine things in life were top of the list for this indulgent Goddess and the same holds true for those born under this sign. They love the finer things in life, from food and drink to fine art. They are tactile, sensual and enjoy immersing themselves in all sensual aspects of life.

Unlike Aries, which precedes Taurus, the people born under this sign enjoy the rewards that life has to offer. Aries enjoy playing the game and aren't that interested in the rewards, while Taureans fully make up for that! Their approach to achieving the good things in life is where we might find the 'bullishness'. They can be slow, steady and ponderous, doggedly pursing their goals in life. This can, on occasion, be interpreted as stubbornness and that interpretation can be a fair one. Those born under this sign will, once set on a course, be hard to move from it. However, they'll almost certainly get there in the end, simply removing obstacles as required until they have achieved that comfortable, luxurious life of plentiful rest and physical pleasure required by their natures.

This may sound self-indulgent but those born with the sun in Taurus will work hard to achieve those spoils. Many can doggedly work for years without apparent reward before achieving that lifestyle. They'll certainly surround themselves in rewards when they reach their goal but, after all the hard work to get there, they'll certainly deserve to do so. They are characteristically practical, resilient and reliable people; if they've said they'll do something they will, however long it takes!

Peace, tranquility and harmony are especially important to Taureans. This applies to all areas of their lives but in particular to their home lives. They value stability and comfort equally; as partners this manifests as a strong desire to please, to provide for and to cherish their mate. The downside to this can be that a Taurus partner can be almost oppressive and potentially clingy. One thing that Taureans need to be aware of is that they can be too possessive but this is a trait that they often seem to be very aware of and manage well, in order to maintain that balance and harmony that they need in their home-lives.

Taurus is fixed sign, along with Leo, Scorpio and Aquarius. These signs are known for their determined qualities and their incredibly strong will power. Taureans are capable of great achievements in life and will work long and hard with determination and little outside support to move whatever obstacles they encounter in life. As an earth sign, they are particularly well grounded; they're not fanciful and will always set realistic goals (their goals may seem unrealistic to others who don't display the same resilience and determination).   Taureans work on facts, reality and practicality and their achievements are built on solid foundations.

Down to earth is a good description of Taurus and when it comes to sports they'll happily engage in mountaineering, hiking or anything that keeps them out in the fresh air and close to the earth that is such a big part of their sign. In terms of stamina Taureans could be said to define the word, long distance treks or endurance sports are perfect ways for them to wile away a day or two (weeks for preference).

Love Life and the Bull

Deeply sensual, loving and faithful, these bullish creatures make excellent partners. Their desire to create a harmonious life at home is a great asset but it can also be something of a downside. They'll go out of their way to create a comfortable, luxurious home for their partner but they can put materialistic considerations over emotional ones on occasion. If you like being constantly showered with gifts a bull may be for you! In terms of the best matches with other Zodiac signs, Scorpio, Virgo and Capricorn are good matches for Taurus. Stability and harmony are also particularly important for the latter of these two, which makes them perfect life partners for the Taurus. Scorpio can be wilder on occasion but this will appeal to many Taureans! Zodiac matches to avoid include Aries, Sagittarius and Gemini. Aries/Taurus can work well together initially, sharing strong-willed and enthusiastic characteristics but long term most Aries will be bored by the 'plodding' nature of the Bull! Sagittarians are often too free spirited and flighty for a Taurean to cope with for long, while Gemini is a restless sign, which will not offer the peace and tranquility that those born under Taurus require.

Career Building the Bovine Way

Taureans are brilliant at making abstract concepts reality. Their natural pragmatism is what is often needed to take wild ideas and turn them into real possibilities. Those born under

Aries may come up with the plan but be unable to see it through to completion. A Taurus, however, will meticulously plan out all the steps required to put pretty much any plan into action. They also have the commitment and stamina to see it through to the end, ensuring a successful outcome. It's also important to remember that Venus rules this sign, so those born under it will have a strong aesthetic sense. This can make them creative and they often thrive well in this type of career.

Taurus characteristics can be useful in a whole range of careers; they make great Executives, capable of leading and mentoring others. As chefs they'll often excel, as this career appears to their love of all things beautiful and sensual. Anything involving the earth, from farming to mineralogy, is likely to capture this bullish earth sign's imagination, while they'll be happy in roles as diverse as interior designer (they love shape, color and texture) to architect (combining design and practical skills). Ultimately a Taurus will work hard at whatever career they choose but those involving problem solving combined with a creative touch will be the most appealing careers.

Gemini, The Twins. A Split Personality?

May 21 – June 20

The Twins – Split personality or dual-core energy? Well, with this sign it might be something of both! From the outside Gemini people can be seen to be flighty, quick to act and impulsive. They're garrulous types and love to chatter on about anything and everything.   It can be difficult to determine just how a Gemini is likely to react in a situation; they could go one way or the other, quite literally.

Gemini is ruled by the planet Mercury, the messenger God of ancient times. Fleet of foot and always on the go, Gemini is an Air sign and one of the mutable signs of the Zodiac. Air is related to thought, intellect and ideas, which are the basic characteristics of this sign. Geminis love to explore the world around them intellectually; they can talk perhaps better than any of the signs but this is no idle chatter, rather it tends to be well thought-out argument and opinion.   Constantly searching for information (especially *new* information) they can seem nosy, prurient and even down-right intrusive. However, this trait is about understanding and Geminis really understand the art of communication, including the listening part of that skill. Whatever information comes their way a Gemini will quickly rationalize it. Like the messenger god symbolized by the planet that rules the sign, Geminis are quick witted, fun and excitable. They're rarely inclined to keep that information to themselves but will happily share it with anybody and everybody around them. This makes them equally great gossips or great intellectuals and teachers. Having Geminis in your life can be a double-edge sword but always makes for an interesting life!

Geminis love people (the source of information) as much as they love information. This makes them generous, caring and sociable creatures; they'll be the life and soul of nearly every party going but they are also extremely good in one-to-one situations, being capable listeners and solvers of problems. The latter, problem solving, in an intellectual sense, is one of their key skills. For anybody with a problem to solve, take a Gemini to one side and talk it over with them; you might get two solutions but each will be equally well thought out.

The constant search for information, for news, for newness, makes Gemini people restless souls. They love travel, sightseeing and learning. Although they love to challenge their minds intellectually they'll also be happy when learning from experiences. Sudden trips to the other side of the world and immersing themselves in very different cultures is something that most Geminis will fearlessly and regularly aim to make part of their lives!

The duality of Gemini has its downsides; they can be moody, or rather very changeable. Sudden and unexpected changes of plans are not unusual with people who are ruled by this sign. To others these can seem almost inexplicable (and even a sign of shallowness) but once you understand that this is just part of the deal with a Gemini it can be easier to cope with. A mutable sign, Gemini is open to change and very capable of dealing with it. The duality of their nature also makes them good at multi-tasking. Geminis can juggle projects like no other sign and while they rarely like to take the lead in any area of life they are valuable team members or family members who can cope with dealing with several issues at one time.

Those born under this sign exhibit a youthful energy and a mercurial one. They can be quick to rise to challenges and quick to initiate new ideas. They're certainly one of the most sociable of signs, with a tendency to flit from one group of friends to another, from one party to the next. Curious about life and very clever, Geminis tend to be popular amongst a wide set of people and posses seemingly boundless amounts of   energy.

Loving Two Halves

Boundless energy and enthusiasm for life, garrulous, inquisitive and flighty; Geminis can be hard to keep in one place! The downside to this is the fact that Geminis don't always exhibit a long attention span and in relationships this can be damaging! Boundless enthusiasm can lead to a sudden and exciting romance for Geminis but their tendency to become bored can lead to heartbreak for the object of their desires when somebody new comes along. Understanding what makes a Gemini tick can help! They often mimic their partners in order to get close and understand them, most Geminis will be constantly analyzing you! "Stay interesting" is the technique to deploy.

Good partners for Geminis include those who have a strong intellectual fascination with the world around them. Bringing new information home for a Gemini each and every day or exploring new ideas and places together will help to create the mix of stability and inspiration that they need. Zodiac matches that work best for Geminis include Libra, Aquarius and Leo. The first two, in particular, are likely to keep a Gemini engaged on a long term basis. The most unlikely matches for Gemini are Taurus, whose simple, steady approach to life will prove too boring for them and Cancer, again, stable, domestic and safety loving.

Mia Rose

Career Juggling

Geminis are very much the intellectuals of the Zodiac but intellectual in both the academic and the emotional sense. They make excellent teachers and lecturers, simply because of their boundless enthusiasm when it comes to knowledge (both learning and imparting it). As they are great communicators and problem solvers they'll also be suited to counseling and psychiatric careers. Geminis love a puzzle and solving it, whether that's complex mathematics or complex personalities. Despite their natural 'flighty' qualities they're also very caring individuals which makes them ideally suited to this type of profession.

Geminis don't particularly take to leadership roles (where consistency and reliability are required) but they do make good team members. They'll be innovative in thought and supportive within a group. They can be extremely important at managing relationships in teams, spotting issues quickly and naturally working to smooth these effortlessly. Jobs and careers which involve change, frequent travel or innovation are ideal. Geminis can be found in many creative careers, particularly those which involve acting and place them firmly center stage.

Cancer, the Crab. Hard Shelled or Soft Centered?

June 22nd – July 22nd

Soft centered and hard shelled; that's a Cancerian for you! The fourth sign of the Zodiac is Cancer, symbolized by the Crab, ruled by the moon and one of the four cardinal signs. There is much in this sig, that is contradictory and this is the key to understanding them. While they're known as the home-bodies of the Zodiac (and they certainly prize home above all else), Cancer people are not adverse to being innovative and vital. The symbol of this sign is easy to understand on many levels; they carry their home with them and this is true of a typical Cancerian. Home, roots, tradition, safety, stability and security are all essential ingredients in life for the happy Cancerian. What is often overlooked is that Cancer the Crab really does carry that home with it. As long as these individuals feel rooted and secure they can be very adventurous indeed, traveling happily and adapting to new people and experiences. "Home, for a Cancerian, can be as much a concept, or a loved one, as it is bricks and mortar. Emotionally strong, think "home is where the heart is" to more fully understand this aspect of Cancer.

Cancerians tend to value family extremely highly; ruled by the moon, the mother-goddess symbol for many cultures, Cancer individuals do like to produce large families, furnish safe nests for them and (occasionally) find it hard to let go of these! Within the family they'll also be the upholder of traditions and the keeper of family lore. Cancer people are never happier than when seated around their (large) kitchen tables, with their (large) families, eating (large) home-cooked meals!

Being ruled by the moon also has another side and this is a moody nature. Those ruled by Cancer can be quick to feel slighted and will retreat into that shell just as quickly. They actually need to spend a certain amount of time alone, in the peace and quiet of their shell, and will find it difficult to be sociable all of the time. This is one of the big contradictions of Cancer the Crab, home and family loving in the extreme and yet private and emotional on occasion. Understanding that your cancer earth-mother (or father) needs time and space on occasion is crucial in your dealings with them. For those born under this sign, knowing that "me-time" is essential to keep your batteries re-charged is also equally important.

That soft centered emotional nature is also often misinterpreted and the hard outer shell is sometimes overlooked. Cancerians can take a lot of knocks in life in their stride; the shell protects them from some knocks that might even have the more obstinate signs reeling. Cancerians are survivors and, although they may retreat once in a while, they keep on going through life with remarkable tenacity. Crab like, they may keep on going sideways though! Cancerians don't often like to confront things head on; they'll avoid direct conflict, scuttling carefully around problems and issues if necessary. While some signs, (like Taurus) may force their way through obstacles a Cancerian will look for a route round them.

Cancers can be prone to brooding in that shell but they can also strike out with those sharp, strong claws. This will nearly always be done in defense of their loved ones, or their home, but that nip can be fatal if you cross them. Ruled by the moon and a water sign, emotions can play a big part in the life of the Cancer born. They can be deeply loving and nurturing but also prone to self-pity and melancholy.

When it comes to sports any team game gets the Cancer 'protective' nature going. However, ideally, Cancerians seek out water for exercise so swimming, water polo or anything which involves immersing themselves in their second home is likely to float their boat! Exercise is also extremely effective at dispelling the occasional dark mood but Cancerians sometimes have to be coaxed out of doors! If you are born under this sign, knowing that exercise can help to manage your emotions is an important way in which to manage them.

Coupling for Crustaceans

Cancer people need stability in their home lives and they also need a partner willing to live within a big family. Their tendency to withdraw into that shell from time to time can make them seem cold and uncaring, while their fierce protectiveness of home and family can seem suffocating on occasion. Cancers can be moody at times and need a partner that can cope with this; ideal partners are Capricorn (an eminently stable and also a family loving sign), Scorpio (dominant but well suited to a caring partner) and Pisces. Pisceans have a similar depth of feeling to Cancerians which can make them particularly suitable. In terms of long term relationships Cancers should avoid settling down early. Contradictory as this may seem, their over-enthusiastic nesting nature can be damaging to them personally. Cancers need to live in the world a little to avoid becoming trapped in the home, having interests and pursuits outside of the home is essential and marriages/partnerships that start in their thirties are often the best option for Cancerians.

Career? What Career?

Career? Cancers would generally prefer to stay home and make their home and families their career. However, their nurturing natures make them excellent carers, nurses and teachers. They're particularly good at teaching younger children and working in environments where a high level of care is needed. Their deeply protective natures also make them good at working with vulnerable groups and they can make powerful advocates for groups in society who need support and security. Cancer individuals will work tirelessly in these settings but must remember that "me-time" is essential for them to avoid burning out and becoming ineffective in whatever field they have chosen. Cancer is a sign that will give and give until they reach exhaustion but remaining effective means learning to manage this trait.

Mia Rose

Leo, the Lion. A Roaring Success?

July 23rd – August 22nd

In ancient times, the sun was considered to be the center of the universe and those born under the sign of Leo, ruled by the Sun, would still largely agree on this fact. As far as Leo's are concerned they are, very much, center stage. You can't normally miss a Leo, they're big, they bound and they roar. Leos have presence!   Ambitious and packed full of enthusiasm and ambition those ruled by this sign have little trouble in making themselves heard, felt and otherwise getting noticed!

This enthusiasm is often backed up by incredible amounts of talent; Leos tend to excel in whatever field they choose – although they'll invariably choose a field which will get them seen. The stage, the screen the talent show, Leos are likely to be there displaying themselves with gusto. With a dramatic outlook on life they also regularly display a real talent for the dramatic and it's no coincidence that many actors and actresses across the centuries have been born under the sign of Leo the Lion.

When it comes to getting things done in life, those born under the influence of this sign also excel. They have a natural dignity and strength of character that marks them out as leaders and as authoritative and powerful individuals.

Leadership, in particular, comes naturally to a Leo and they'll happily take them helm of anything that comes their way – be that a small company or a large country. Key qualities that Leos display are their talents for being organized, their strong idealism and their ability to inspire others. Having a natural sense that they were born to rule (in whatever context) Leos can come across as domineering, overbearing and even dictatorial. To some extent they are, but they use these skills to see things through and get things done. A fixed sign they can be inflexible but they are also determined. It's rarely advisable to get in the way of a Leo, once they have set their course!

Self-assurance is another central quality of the Leo personality and, on the whole, they put this confidence to good use. While tending to see themselves as the center of the universe they also believe that they are indispensable to those around them. This can actually be true – having a Leo in your life will certainly remove most obstacles. Others may view Leos as self-important, vain or just plain bossy but Leos themselves regard this as nonsense. Leos also have a very strong sense of loyalty to those around them or to projects with which they are involved. Not only can you count on a Leo to get things done, you can count on them to do those things in the best interests of those they are working with.

Their regal nature makes Leos value peace; they dislike strife, discordancy and unrest. While they expect everyone to follow their lead they do understand the importance of the greater good and the greater happiness and this makes them (to some) surprisingly good negotiators. While most Leos will be confident that they are right, this doesn't stop them from listening to other points of view and to finding a consensus or a common ground. Leos want peace, harmony and good times, they don't like civil war or revolutions. Although capable of enforcing their will on others they're well aware that consensus is the way to rule and they will make great efforts to achieve this.

Royal Weddings

Leos love to be in charge and Kings don't always make great husbands (as any of the six wives of Henry VIII would be willing to tell you). Male or female Leos like power, they expect to be in charge and are often surprised when partners don't entirely agree on this. Young Leos often need to learn that negotiation is a part of life (including in personal relationships) and this means that they can work their way through a string of relationships before developing the art of compromise. On the upside Leos can be intensely loyal, caring and protective but, in general, are better at developing quality long-term relationships later in life. This doesn't have to mean in their dotage but certainly into their thirties and forties. This is also a time of life where they have often achieved significant power and influence in other areas of their life – which can mean they don't tend to be quite so controlling at home!

In terms of Zodiac compatibility other fire signs are often the best choice, including enthusiastic and youthful Aries or fiery but philosophical Sagittarius. Aquarius, a water sign, is the opposite of Leo and yet, oddly, these two opposites seem to attract. Sharing ideals in life, if not approaches, this relationship can create a perfect balance.

Pride of (Work) Place

Leos ideal and most suitable career choice should be King (or Queen). They'll settle for President, if they live in a republic, but ultimately they're aware of their own natural abilities as leaders. In the real world this translates as the ideal personality for company CEO, or local/regional political leader. Leos will, apparently effortlessly, climb their way to positions of power and influence and can easily manage running a country or two. They will however, be happy in many political or leadership roles and their natural leadership abilities, along with their sometimes overlooked negotiation skills, make them perfect for these roles. These negotiation skills also make them excellent diplomats or negotiators and Leos can make startlingly successful sales people if the need arises.

If political or corporate openings are lacking, the other field in which Leos find themselves completely at home is on the stage or screen. They have such a commanding presence that the stage is, in fact, perfect for them. Being center of attention, or top of the pile, is important to Leos and they thrive in these circumstances; menial jobs or jobs in which they have to take subordinate roles are rarely suitable.

Virgo, the Virgin. Modest to a Fault?

August 23rd – September 22nd

Self-deprecating, modest, humble and full of humility. Virgo, represented by the symbol of the Virgin, could be said to be all of these. It could also said to be exacting, precise and deeply spiritual. Virgin, in ancient times, did not have the same, or quite the same, meaning as it does in the modern, Western world. In Rome, the Vestal Virgins were a sect dedicated to Vesta, the goddess of the hearth (and by implication the home) but also dedicated to the protection of the city itself. Virgins were, in many ancient cultures, women who were freed from normal social obligations to devote themselves to study and ritual. To understand the qualities of Virgo these concepts are essential.

Those ruled by this sign are often deeply analytical, displaying an attention to detail that is mind-boggling to others. They are also known for their desire to serve and their extremely strong abilities at this. They have an inborn sense of duty to both serve and defend and, in the case of many Virgos, this is very much in the ancient sense of serving and defending the state.

Ancient 'virgins' were deeply devoted to study and ritual; the sign Virgo is intrinsically involved with these activities. Ancient Vestal Virgins could interpret complex signs, symbols and portents in anything from entrails to complex legal documents. When it comes to examining and interpret complex details or data in the modern world a Virgo is your man (or woman). They are practical and logical at the same time, they analyze (everything) and then interpret their analysis in detail. Virgos don't make rash judgments or emotional ones; they make decisions based on learned facts. If you need something done right, first time, then call in the nearest Virgo; just don't expect it done quickly.

An earth sign, Virgos display a very strong, grounded rooted and practical approach to life. They are ruled by the planet Mercury, like the twins Gemini, and this makes them highly intellectual and - on occasion - mercurial in mood. These mercurial mood swings are, however, more tempered in aspect than with the flighty Gemini. They have strong critical abilities which they apply to every area of their lives, from work to personal relationships. Above all Virgos love understanding how things work and they work on the principle that this can be applied to atomic engineering and/or spouses!

Virgos are sometimes seen as picky, in both relationships and in material areas of their lives. They do like to surround themselves with 'quality' objects and possessions and they also enjoy deep, fulfilling relationships. They can be as picky about their interior design as their friends and partners which sometimes means they are accused of coldness – in fact this is simply practical analysis in action and their choices are invariably made on a sound basis and create long lasting results.

Love under Examination

Living with a Virgo can feel like being under a microscope. They need to understand you on just about every level and while this can create a very strong relationship – given that they also have a very strong need to serve – it can also be stifling for some people. Virgos are not often swept off their feet by wild romances, tending to way the pros, cons and potential fiscal renumeration involved in a future relationship. They can also be shy, humble and undervalue their own abilities, all of which can make the Virgos search for love a long one. On the other hand a Virgo's natural tendency to look long and hard before leaping can mean that their relationships are long lasting. Ideal matches in the Zodiac include Capricorn (often passionately analytical themselves), Taurus (all heart but appreciative of your intellectual stance on life) and Pisces (the opposite sign which compliments your own abilities and balances them incredibly well!).

Forensic Examinations

Interviewing a Virgo, unless you are one, is a terrifying experience. They'll reverse the process before you know what has happened. With a microscopic attention to detail, and deeply analytical in their approach, Virgos can be found making successful careers in everything from administration to molecular science. It doesn't matter what the job is to many Virgos, simply getting it right is the most important thing. They have a strong sense of duty to the wider community and this makes them particularly happy working in medical research settings, which allow them to indulge their twin abilities of infinitely detailed research and a wider usefulness to society.

Virgos work well as administrators in government settings and with strong communication abilities can also work well in political roles. Their need to serve can even take them into a military field, although they'll prefer to do so in a logistical or medical setting, serving in a way that involves protecting those around them. Similarly careers in forensic sciences within law enforcement, or even pathology, will suit the deeply analytical, fact based skills of the Virgo.

Libra, the Scales. A Balancing Act?

September 23rd – October 22nd

Balance, poise, elegance and justice; all things that are associated with the symbol representing this sign of the zodiac. The symbol in itself deserves some scrutiny in this case – unlike the other symbols of the zodiac this a sign represented by something man-made. While the other signs depict animals, and a few depict human or mythological creatures, the Libran scales suggest crafted artifice. In some respects this aspect of the sign is apparent in those born under its influence.

Those with the Sun in Libra love all things beautiful and crave harmony and balance in all areas of life. Their love of the good things in life, be that art, music or attractive people, is largely down to the ruler of the sign, Venus. Goddess of love, beauty and pleasure; for Libran their ruler's preoccupation with beauty and pleasure is pronounced but, true to the symbol of the sign, all of these must be in balance. An air sign, Librans can seem aloof, intellectual and almost elitist. It's true that their tastes are refined, that thought and intellect is important to them, but they also have a strong sense of justice and fairness and this, combined with their other qualities more often makes them cultured but sensitive individuals.

Like the set of scales that symbolizes their sign, Librans operate best in life when their whole life is in balance. They seek equal partnerships in romance and in their careers and the former is extremely important to them. Partnership to them is a word that has a capital P and this extends fully into their home lives. They'll tolerate neither a submissive partner nor one who demands to be in control. Librans, perhaps above all signs, seek to mate for life and, no doubt thanks to their profound sense of justice and equality, often succeed in creating a lasting bond.

Librans need balance in all areas of their lives and are excellent communicators, thanks to their qualities as an air sign. They dislike conflict in the extreme, as this is a cause of imbalance. They negotiate their way through life but not from fickleness or indecisiveness (as it is sometimes seen) but through genuine needs for establish an equilibrium in their lives and the people around them. Their techniques at achieving this balance can be seen as an expression of vanity or of a gossipy nature and Librans should beware of this trait. They are genuinely charming and great conversationalists but their need to please everyone all the time can lead to unfair accusations of two-facedness or falseness. Peace, is what Librans crave, not discord.

Natural strategists in all areas of life Librans are great negotiators. They'll organize everyone and everything to make sure any group works to the best of its abilities. This is a massively valuable trait in many areas of life. Librans have excellent intuition at spotting the right person for a task, persuading that person that they are the right person for the task and then negotiating with others to ensure the right tools for the task are in place. If you need a country invading, and have limited resources, appoint the nearest Libran as your Chief-of- Staff. If everything goes wrong (which is unlikely) then get them to negotiate the peace deal. In discussion and argument a Libra will rarely take offense, they combine their powers of communication, deliberation and need for balance and will consider all points of view logically and with fairness.

Equal Partners – Love and the Libran

Amiable, accommodating and with a strong desire to build a lasting relationship based on love, affection and equality. Librans sound like the perfect partner in many respects. As an air sign they can intellectualize relationships a little too much for some but they're passionate and love beauty and companionship. Aries, the opposite Zodiac sign, compliments Libra perfectly. Librans value the straightforward no-nonsense attitude that the youthful Ram encapsulates. This combination of the two rulers, Venus and Mars, makes for a great compliment of qualities, enthusiasm, creativity, aggression and tenderness. Gemini, another dual sign, works well with Libra too, both understand the others duality well and this can make for a well balanced match.

Aquarians with their love of beauty and life in general, will also make for a comfortable partnership. The least likely matches with Libra are Scorpio, the sting in their tale can tip the scales out of balance for weeks at a time and Virgo, who are, in most Librans opinions, to obsessed with fine details when a general consensus would do!

Organized Futures

Librans make excellent administrators, negotiators and logistical professionals. Their strong sense of fairness and justice means that they'll thrive in organizations which help those less well off in society. Charity and NGO work is perfect for them, especially where their skills at management or negotiation can be deployed to the full. They also make good counselors, either on a one to one level or for couples or groups. Fund-raising roles also appeal to their natural negotiation and fairness needs while they also work extremely well, deploying their bountiful amounts of charm, in public relations roles. Working in the arts, particularly in arts promotion, is also an attractive option which will provide them with opportunities to enjoy their cultured, aesthetic side to the full.

Scorpio, the Scorpion. A Controlling Freak?

October 23rd – November 21st

When threatened with imminent danger the Scorpion will happily use its own sting to kill itself. This doesn't mean that those ruled by this sign are a suicidal bunch but it does demonstrate the Scorpion need to be in control Yes, meet the control freak of the Zodiac! In the case of Scorpio this control is about controlling their own destiny and not necessarily everybody else around them.

Like the insect that symbolizes this sign, those born with the Sun in Scorpio are also an inquisitive lot; they'll scuttle here and there, back and forth, in search of information. They're also very adept at getting straight to the point and don't mess around with chatter and small talk. You can always spot a Scorpio in a crowd simply from their directness. They also exhibit an alarmingly strong sense of intuition which means that they unerringly ask the right questions (though not always at the right time as others may perceive it) to find the answer to whatever they wish to know.

Pushy may not be the word to describe Scorpio. That strong desire to control their own destiny often means that Scorpio's agenda is the only agenda as far as they are concerned. They will rarely negotiate, or discuss or consider the impact on others (unless that impact affects them too). Straight to the point and deadly if necessary, Scorpios work hard and play hard in order to create the perfect environment for themselves.

In the ancient world the sign was considered to be ruled by Mars, the God of War, adept at fighting for a cause. In recent history the sign is also considered to be ruled by Pluto, the shadowy, dark God of the Underworld. This adds a depth of awareness to the motivated and active Scorpio and those born under its influence often seem to have an intuition that is almost a sixth sense. This makes Scorpio a powerful adversary or an indispensable ally. Scorpions can have hot tempers and can be quick to react when crossed with a powerful streak of vindictive fury. An angry Scorpio individual is best given plenty of room!

There is, however, another side to Scorpio and this is explained by its element, which is eater. In the case of Scorpio these waters run deep. Unlike other water signs where emotions are clear, the strong, silent emotional tides of those born under the sign are quiet but desperately strong. They are equally emotional as those born under other water signs but they'll never show it willingly; all that energy is pent up and can on occasion, boil over. More often though, their strong emotions combine with their strong wills, creating a powerful and passionate personality which can move mountains if it deems necessary. The mystical elements of Water and the presence of Pluto as a signs ruler will also often lead Scorpios away from worldly considerations and down the path of spiritual or mystical exploration. Their ability to understand the depths of human emotion, their keen sense of intuition and their direct approach to problem solving can make this route beneficial not only for them as individuals but for many others around them.

Love Hurts

It's not me, it's you. If you're going to hear these words from anyone, it'll be a Scorpio. Direct and to the point, Scorpios can make some others quail under their honesty and scrutiny, though many find their direct honesty deeply refreshing. Scorpios can be dark creatures and appear lonely but the fact is that they are patient types who have the stamina to search for many years until they find the perfect partner. Their depth of emotional intuition means that they'll know straight away when they've found that person and it's this emotional connection which will be valued most by their partners. They'll know if you've had a bad day before you do and they'll already have created the perfect environment to make it right. Scorpios aren't that interested in simplicity and this means that they are happy to accept and accommodate other's complexity.

While they'll respond rapidly to your emotions, Scorpios will often hide their own, this can seem to be 'sulking' but it's usually best to let them have time to brood. The obvious, perfect match for Scorpios are those born under the sign of

Cancer; hard shells, soft, emotionally charged centers? Need we say more? It just works. Scorpios and Virgos both work hard and also work well together and their abilities, directness and analysis complement each other extremely well. Piscean/Scorpio love matches work well, but Pisces can be possessive and this can leave Scorpio feeling trapped and lashing out violently. Neither Aries nor Gemini work well with Scorpio – they simply see life too simply and with too much youthful enthusiasm for Scorpio. Aries people also like to be in control – as do Scorpios - and this tends to lead to direct confrontation.

Battle Stations

Scorpios are decision makers extraordinaire but not in a rash way. They use intellect, evidence and gut instinct, which makes them perfect investigators. The subject under investigation can vary; from police work to psychology. Their ability to control their emotions combined with a deep empathy suits them well to the latter work and their complete lack of fear when it comes to complexity and contradiction can make them excellent psychoanalysts. In the corporate world, if you want an 'out of the box' thinker, then find a Scorpio. They're probably not aware of the box unless the solution is inside it. Scorpios can also work extremely well in PR situations – particularly disaster management as they instinctively know how to protect and fight for their own interests.

The Scorpio's ruthlessness, combined with their ability to analyze, can also make them successful in military roles. Scorpios will kill, both literally and figuratively, in order to defend with no hesitation.

Sagittarius, the Archer. Crazy Horses?

November 22nd – December 21st

"Don't fence me in"; this could easily be the motto of the Sagittarian. The symbol of this sign is commonly recognized as the Archer but this is slightly inaccurate and misleading to the modern mind. The symbol that represents this ninth sign of the Zodiac is actually a Centaur Archer, half-man, half-horse. These mythical creatures have long been associated with the 'wanderer' perhaps a mythological representation of the nomadic tribes of mysterious Asia encountered by early Greek explorers. Even today, the wild horsemen and women of tribes like the Altai can inspire the feeling that the riders and the horse are one creature. Sagittarius is the symbol of both the wanderer and the seeker and this interpretation of the sign offers a better understanding of the true nature of those born with Sagittarius as their ruler.

Sagittarians seek truth and, for them, the simplest way to find it is to explore the world around them. In their own hearts they know that this exploration cannot be localized, they need to hit the road, or preferably many of them, to find the truths they are seeking. They are exceptionally clear thinkers (the archer here, symbolizing directness and incisiveness) and the Centaur was considered to represent the intellectual in ancient times. They think, examine, talk and debate; these qualities can, on occasion, lead to accusations of bluntness and it's true that Sagittarians like others to agree with their opinions.

Sagittarius is, however, a mutable sign and that quality makes those born under the sign keenly open to listening. How else would you learn, is their opinion! They love information, the more the better, in order to evaluate every and any argument until that ever elusive 'truth' can be established. The passion for finding the truth can lead to stubbornness; once a Sagittarian has found "the truth" they rarely let go. They'll have evaluated the facts and have come to their conclusion and here the stubbornness that is typical of the horse-half of the Centaur kicks in.

Jupiter is the ruler of this sign and also the ancient Roman ruler of the Gods. This tends to give Sagittarians an air of leadership and authority; to them this feels natural and to others the sense of leadership often inspires a strong need to follow. To those born under impulsive, independent signs it can, however, feel domineering and dictatorial. Fire is the element that is associated with Sagittarius and in this sense its the quick thinking, rapidly moving elements of fire that we see. Sagittarians have quick minds but can also be prone to flitting from one thought, or subject, to the next. Fire, stubbornness and strength can all be useful qualities but they can also leave a trail of destruction in their path. An out-of-control Sagittarian can likewise be damaging to those around them. However, given the space to roam and inquire that they need, the opportunity to lead (which they enjoy doing for the greater good) and plenty of food for thought, a Sagittarian will remain happy, peaceful and a powerful ally.

Saddled for Life?

Impetuous, inquisitive and with a tendency (a strong need in fact) to roam, Sagittarians are not, it has to be admitted, ideal partners for everybody. They can be easily distracted and you may have to play (apparent) second best to a host of other interests and people. Living with and loving a Sagittarian means accepting the half-wild part of their soul. They're not great on social conventions, they may prove unwilling to settle down until later in life and they'll nearly always need far more intellectual stimulation than any one individual can provide. Signs which are best mated with Sagittarians include Aries and Leo, both are fire signs which work well with the passion and quick thinking displayed by Sagittarius. Leo and Sagittarius work particularly well together, both being naturally regal and, as Ferdinand and Isabella proved so efficiently, two crowned heads can be better than one when it comes to taking over the world. Cancer, home loving and emotionally sensitive rarely makes a good match for the open-road needing Sagittarius, while Virgos can be so meticulous they'll spend a lot of time fixing the bolt on the stable door only to discover the inevitable too late.

Traveling Representatives

If you combine the concept of travel, evaluation and sharing ideas and then see what you get, you'll probably have the perfect mix for a Sagittarius's career; a travel writer. This sort of work ticks most of the boxes for Sagittarians. Open roads, the chance to explore ideas and then share them will always work for Sagittarians; they also make great motivational speakers, researchers (not office based though) and investigative journalists.

There is also a deeply spiritual side to Sagittarians so quests of this nature will appeal and they'll make great missionaries with both the passion and physical stamina to adapt to this sort of lifestyle.

As ambassadors Sagittarians can be successful, they see the broad picture and communicating is like breathing for them. However, detailed diplomacy is not their greatest skill as details can bore them and negotiating is not always a concept that comes easily to them. Careers which involve limited variety are deadly to Sagittarians so anything monotonous and repetitive should be avoided.

Capricorn, the Goat. Don't Get Trampled!

December 22nd – January 19th

Determined, plodding and ambitious. The tenth sign of the Zodiac is symbolized by Capricorn, the goat, but you won't find many Capricorns bleating plaintively through life. There are a number of misconceptions about this sign, which like Sagittarius has a slightly deeper meaning in ancient mythology than is recognized by modern minds. Goats are tenacious and adaptable, they'll eat (read "try") anything once on the off-chance it might be palatable (read "lead to success") and they may occasionally get stuck in difficult situations. However, turn your back for a minute and they'll have extricated themselves from what seemed an impossible place.

This symbol of the Zodiac, however, has another side and this particular goat has something fishy about it; the mythological beast was, in fact, the sea-goat and this watery side, mystical, emotional and on occasion, dangerously wild, is the side that many modern astrologers choose to ignore. In addition, Capricorn also shares a mythological origin with Bacchus and the Saturnalian. Again, this doesn't fit well with our image of the sober, steadfast, plodding ascent of the old goat. Wild parties, orgies and unrestrained passions, all behind that mild-mannered Machiavellian suit? Oh, yes. Capricorns are very private people, but for those few individuals that they let in on the secret, a party is waiting.

The goat is the worker of the Zodiac, striving onwards and upwards through sheer hard labor throughout their lives. Capricorns tend to take the slow (very thorough) route to success. It's the overlooked side of their character (the intuition brought by the influences of water in the guise of that fishy tail) that often helps them to achieve those great heights. A little like Scorpio, these waters run deep and you won't see a Capricorn express much emotion. That would be wasteful and unproductive, but it doesn't mean they aren't sensitive to the world around them, intuitive about other's emotions and not entirely unhurt by slights. Possessed with a hard head and a set of horns, when crossed or finding an obstacle in their way, they aren't afraid to bash through. On the way to the top, the goat is not afraid to knock people out of the way.

Capricorns are ruled by Saturn and the sign is an earth sign. Saturn, according to mythology, was the father of the Gods and they often exhibit strict, paternalistic attitudes. They are conservative in their attitudes but (thanks to the element of earth) are grounded in reality and practicality. While respectful of tradition and convention they aren't afraid to head-butt it out of the way if it's no longer useful (or in their way). This is a trait that is often overlooked in those born under this sign but goes a long way to explain their preeminence amongst not only great leaders but also great revolutionaries. Capricorns like to get to the top of the mountain and are prepared to be polite in order to do so; they're also prepared to employ a firing squad if polite doesn't work.

Capricorn people are extremely hard working and they like things to work properly (success depends on it, after all). This means that they are fastidious in their approach and their attention to detail can be invaluable. They'll work long and hard on any project and they'll see it through to completion, however long that takes. They'll then move on to the next project to complete their ultimate world domination!

Arranged Marriages

Capricorns work at everything and this includes their relationships. Their earth qualities make them passionate and those hidden, watery sides can make them emotionally very complex. However, of all the signs they're the most likely to marry for convenience (advancement).

Capricorns do depend on stability in the home and this means that they tend to value long, lasting and equal relationships when building a home with their partner. They like to plan, to discuss and to resolve, which can be downright boring for some people. However, that wild Bacchanalia side, rarely seen in their public lives, is often reserved for their intimate circles. On the downside Capricorn's work ethic can be hard for some people to live with – most Capricorns will be deeply focused on their career and will make better partners once they've achieved their goal in life.

The opposite sign of Cancer makes for a perfect match for Capricorn, Cancerians need stability and a home to furnish; Capricorns will work to provide for this home and will offer the stability and loyalty that Cancer craves. The watery side of both signs means they can find a deep compatibility on an emotional level too. Virgo's appreciate Capricorns perfectionism and this match can make for an effective personal and business relationship. Both signs like hard work and unlike most couples, working together in this case can lead to success in both love and career.

Which Job?

The top job is the one for a Capricorn. However, they won't be satisfied with being parachuted in. Capricorns actually need to work from the ground up. They'll probably trample a few people on the way but they appreciate getting to know the terrain – making it easier to control once they're up there. There are actually few areas of work that a Capricorn won't be happy in, they enjoy the process of rising to the top of any career, as much as the career itself. They like power, so politics is a field (or mountain) they'll enjoy but their inquisitiveness makes for plenty of potential in journalism too. Capricorns can be an asset in many companies as they value hard work and are never afraid of it. Don't underestimate them though, if you're CEO; they may be an errand boy/girl today, but they *are* after your job. And they'll probably get it.

Aquarius, the Water Carrier. Born to Serve?

January 20th – February 18th.

One of the few signs of the Zodiac symbolized by a (fully) human motif. Bearing and dispensing water, the basic necessity for life, Aquarians are the humanitarians of the Zodiac. Their aim is to create a better world, to provide succor and to ensure that they leave the world a better place than they found it. Philanthropic to the core, the Aquarian thrives on serving those around them and the wider world.

An air sign, Aquarius is motivated through thought as well as action, showering us all with their thoughts. These thoughts are aimed and designed to improve. They are extremely analytical in their approach to life and their desire to solve problems is paramount. Aquarius is often the sign of the genius, the innovator and the inspirer of change (for the better). They are inventive souls who seek to work collaboratively with others to find solutions for all.

At first glance that simple water vessel seems like a very ancient concept and, of course, it is. However to the earliest humans any tool was cutting edge technology and this goes a long way to explaining another characteristic trait of those born under the sign. If it's new, techy, shiny or gadgety among the first people to have it will be a full set of Aquarians. They believe in technology as a way to advance society for the better and they're not afraid to use it. Their natural, often quirky, inventiveness often means they probably had a hand in inventing it anyway but if it's early up-take your looking for, fill your focus group with Aquarians.

Aquarians have strong principles and strong beliefs and are good at articulating both. They can, however, be temperamental and argumentative when crossed. They have a strong sense of 'right' and don't like this to be contradicted, seeming quick to anger and impatient when dealing with those who disagree with them.

Aquarius has two rulers; Saturn and Uranus. Saturn, the father of the Gods gives them a similar parental, conservative approach in life to Capricorns in some sense. They believe that they know best and can adopt a "do as I say, not as I do" approach in some circumstances. The other, more recently identified ruler of the sign is Uranus; the oldest god in Roman mythology and a mysterious shadowy creature from the dawn of time. This connects Aquarians to the vital forces of creation and inspiration and also can attract them to a mystical, esoteric view of the world. They are the innovators, the creators and visionaries of the Zodiac.

Spreading the Love

Those born under the sign of Aquarius value cooperation and love very highly. They are excellent communicators and care deeply about the world and those that they love. Aquarians can love just about everyone so that makes them less easy for those who need to be the center of their partner's attention. However, they are easy going, generous and creative. Aquarians have a vibrant inner life and intellect, which is often the center of their world, for those living with people born under this sign, reminding them to come out and play occasionally is no bad idea. Like Capricorn, they are ruled by Saturn, and when you access the Saturnalian side of your Aquarius, the party is definitely on. Geminis, with their love of unpredictable natures make great partners for Aquarians, while Librans share a love of beauty and perfection with Aquarians – they also like plenty of time alone, which leaves an Aquarius free to dreamily invent a solution to world poverty. Avoid those born under Taurus, Cancer and Virgo; generally they'll need more attention than is available from an Aquarius and Virgo like order, not inventive chaos, in their lives!

Saving the World, One Invention at a Time

Inventive, innovative and highly intellectual, careers in technology will suit most Aquarians. If the invention will save mankind, then all the better, but as long as it's new and amazing, they'll be happy. Careers in science and engineering are excellent choices. Aquarius has a need to change the world for the better though, and politics often attracts them. This can be a good choice later in life, although campaigning for a good cause will often be a part of their lives whatever their main career. Seeking answers to problems, preferably using technology, will suit most born with the Sun in Aquarius and IT is another place where they'll find a comfortable niche.

Pisces, the Fish. Splendid Illusions?

February 19th – March 20th.

Two fish briefly appear at the edge of a pool, their forms shimmering and changing below the surface and then, as quickly as they appear, they're gone. Masters of illusion? Shape shifters? Merely illusions? Timid? Not entirely of this world? Were there even two of them? Welcome to the complex, other-worldly nature of Pisces. This sign is the most "mature" of the Zodiac and, as you may have noticed as we've progressed each sign, each has become more complex, more contradictory and often more elusive. Pisces is a sign that manifest all of these qualities in abundance.

In some senses those born under this sign combine all of the qualities of the other signs of the Zodiac but rarely, if ever, manifest them all. Water, in which they 'live' is a spiritual element and this is the strongest feature that they display. They are a selfless, spiritual bunch, deeply compassionate and yet often focused on their own, inner spiritual journey. The most intuitive of the signs, they are highly sensitive to the feelings and needs of others but this can make them tend to avoid contact with those around them, feeling the emotions (good and bad) that surround them too keenly.

The symbol representing this sign is two fish, not one, and this represents an important aspect of the sign; duality. Like other signs that express this duality Pisceans demonstrate an acute awareness of their own two-sidedness and of the complexity of the 'real' and the 'imaginary'. In fact, to a Piscean, the seen and the unseen are both real and they dwell comfortably in either realm. Their intuitive natures makes them appear psychic and they will often shift and change their natures to fit the people and circumstances around them. This can lead to accusations of being flighty and unreliable or indecisive but is, in fact, an expression of their need to serve others rather than themselves.

Pisceans tend to like their own company – being deeply introspective and happy to examine their own feelings and thought processes. The can often retreat for long periods of time into silent reflection and yet will then come darting back, vibrant, refreshed and willing to give their time to those that they believe need or deserve it. That group is large, as there is a willing self-sacrificing side to this sign, which can make them vulnerable to the less altruistic people.

The planets that rule this sign are Jupiter (traditionally) and Neptune (in more recent times). King of the Gods and King of the Seas, this pair bring a sense of authority to the sign. From Neptune, Pisceans are gifted with a strength but also a terrible unpredictability. Pisceans can be stormy or gentle and nurturing. Their strong sensitivity to other's pain, however, rarely makes them capable of tyranny or of inflicting pain which would, in effect, be self-harm. The average Piscean's ability to live in both a real and fantasy world can lead them to becoming dis-attached from reality; they dream of a perfect life and, unable to distinguish fact from fantasy, can become delusional. Channeled correctly however, this temperament makes them brilliant in certain fields of life, particularly in the creative industries. Artists, writers, filmmakers and actors are often found under this sign.

The Mirror of Love

Pisceans will reflect your needs; they feel them so keenly that those needs become their own, until somebody else passes within a mile or so. This leads to accusations of blowing 'hot and cold' but it's important to understand that it's simply in their nature to empathize. Unlike other water signs, Pisces don't have a shell and their emotions can be very much on the surface and very much open to damage. While Cancer will retreat into its shell and sulk for a while Pisces will be gone, flitting off and almost seemingly never there. Be gentle with a Pisces, or be prepared to lose them.

Pisces have a vibrant inner life and are not beyond making their dreams reality; this can make them unpredictable and may mean sudden, unexpected (for you) changes of lifestyle. Pisceans can be hard to pin down and don't thrive well if they are. On early dates be prepared to make decisions – a Pisces won't know what film they want to see, because they won't know what film you want to see and therefore will have no idea what film they want to see. Get the picture? If you don't like that picture go fishing in other waters!

Fantasy Jobs

Pisceans can dream up their perfect career, visualize it clearly and then live in that dream. The fact that reality and fantasy are much of a muchness for them can make earning real money a challenge for those born under this sign. Actually, they're less interested in the cash than the perfect life, so this may not be a problem. However, any career which enables them to deploy their intense creative energy is a good choice. Fantasy is a world that comes easy to them, so working in films in any role (costume design, set design, acting etc.) is perfect for them. Writing (fiction, not fact) is also a career in which Pisceans can achieve great things.

Pisceans have a strong sense of intuition about what others want and this can make advertising roles a serious possibility for them. While empathetic, Pisceans can take on other's emotions too easily and so although counseling may seem an obvious choice it should be avoided.

Conclusion

Thank you again for reading this book!

I hope this book has given you insight into your own sign of the Zodiac and that of your friends and family and also highlighted some areas which are overlooked in modern Astrology.

Finally, if you enjoyed this book, please take the time to share your thoughts and post a review on Amazon. It'd be greatly appreciated!

Thank you and good luck!

Astral Projection

The Beginners Guide On

How To Travel Out Of Your

Body On The Astral Plane

Written By

Mia Rose

Introduction

I want to thank you and congratulate you for getting the book, "Astral Projection".

This book contains proven steps and strategies on how to practice Astral Projection.

Astral Projection and Out-of-Body-Experiences have been described throughout human history and yet they still remain a mystery to many people. While science remains unclear as to the "how", "why" or even the "if" our mind and soul are separate from the body, many ancient traditions take this as a simple fact. Astral Projection allows you to experience for yourself the wider context of both our physical world and the universe. It will also help you to develop a deeper sense of who you are, your purpose in life and can also help to combat the fear of death itself!

This book takes you through simple steps that anybody can learn to use and will teach you all you need to know to develop strong skills and begin to Project your Astral Body beyond your physical. The book explores techniques, safety tips and the benefits of Astral Projection in a simple to understand and easy to use way.

Thanks again for reading this book, I hope you enjoy it!

Chapter 1

Astral Projection, Near-Death Experiences and What We Know So Far

Astral Projection has been practiced in many different cultures across the world and throughout history. Today it is commonly understood in the context of the "out-of-body-experience" (OOBE). These experiences have been reported by people from all backgrounds and all cultures but current scientific understanding of the phenomenon is limited and science remains skeptical about the truth (or facts) behind either OOBE or Astral Projection.

Astral Projection is a complex subject but in simple terms it can be defined as a belief that as humans we have a physical body and an "Astral body". In most cultures, historically, this has been equated with the spirit or the soul. We are complex beings and science and medicine have made great leaps in understanding how our bodies and brains work in recent decades. However, much is still yet to be understood about the brain, while the spirit, the soul and the mind pose yet greater mysteries.

In terms of the Astral body, those who accept the concept argue that this manifestation of our soul or spirit can travel beyond the physical body, independently of it. There is a strong link, in many traditions, between the concepts of Astral Projection and the concepts of an afterlife, or the existence of realms other than the physical realm in which we live our lives. Astral Projection, OOBE's and even the concept of soul or spirit are controversial subjects. In fact, for centuries philosophers have debated the very nature of humanity and the concept that our soul is a separate entity to the real and physical body. While it's accepted that our soul or spirit is what make us "us", there is no real consensus in where the soul comes from or where it goes after our physical body "wears out".

However, while science lacks much serious research or evidence on the subject there are countless examples of belief systems in which the soul (sometimes called the spirit) is not only acknowledged but is considered a separate and separable form of ourselves. Christianity, Islam, Judaism, Hinduism, Buddhism and many other traditions all accept the existence of the soul. They all, also, accept that this soul exists after our own physical death and many consider it to exist before our births.

Both Hindu and Buddhist traditions are good examples in which the soul is seen as existing before our physical body is created and also after it dies. Both differ, in some respects, but both see the soul itself as a greater entity that is on a journey of learning and enlightenment in which the ultimate aim is to achieve a point where re-birth and re-incarnation is no longer necessary and we become part of a higher entity, existing on a different plane. In nearly every culture that has existed in history this concept of an after-life, or another plane of existence, has existed and can be found in cultures as diverse as Ancient Egyptian right through to the isolated cultures of the Pacific Ocean.

Does the universality of this belief mean that it is real? Science and cynics may argue that it doesn't, while supporters of the concept would argue that it is more than enough proof. However, perhaps the truth is yet to be discovered and perhaps it is a truth that in our own brief lifetimes we may not be able to unravel. The concept is, however, so universal that whatever you believe it cannot be purely coincidence that the concept of planes of existence beyond the visible and physical should appear in all cultures throughout history. It seems more than likely that there is something behind the concept and for those who practice Astral Projection, it is a very clear and present truth.

Near-Death Experiences

Near-Death Experiences, a form OOBE, have been documented throughout history. In the modern world science and medicine have had an impact on the number and frequency of these events. As medical techniques improve "death" is not as arbitrary as it once was and many people are routinely "brought back" from the dead. This has resulted in more reports of near death or OOBE. The individuals concerned report seeing themselves, their physical bodies, from above and often return accurate reports of the room in which that body lies, the medics trying to resuscitate them and many small details that it seems unlikely they could know consciously.

These reports vary in many respects but often include the feeling, sensation or vision of moving towards a bright light, of encountering beings, or relatives who have died. In the case of those that return to report on the event, it's often the case that a voice or figure has told them that they are not ready, it's not their time or their place to be, as yet. There are, in many cases, a startling consistency to these reports. Some medics and scientists are skeptical but others have taken measures to "test" the event, placing objects high in a room that cannot be seen by anyone, least of all a prone, clinically dead patient! The results have, again, suggested that there may be more to our existence than is necessarily understood in terms of a purely physical sense.

The near-death experience is, furthermore, not restricted to those of a religious or spiritual nature. Reports of OOBE have been made by people from all walks of life, all backgrounds and all (and no) religious persuasion. From devout

Christians to confirmed atheists, the near-death experience does not seem to discriminate.

The Universe or Universes?

Despite what you may think, the scientific jury is out on this question and the verdict seems likely to be swinging in favor of the latter! While most scientists seem unwilling to accept the concepts of either an after-life or Astral Projection, the concept of different planes of reality is more problematic for them. Theoretically, they'll admit, that more than one universe is not just possible but very likely indeed. Parallel or multiple universes are considered to be more probable than one single universe. Even the Big Bang Theory (in which everything is created out of nothing) is now under severe scrutiny. Science is beginning to accept that not only is this just a theory, but it's not a very good one! However, the existence of multi-verses is hard to prove and the possibility that we can move from one reality (or universe) to another (a parallel universe) is very far from being proved in scientific terms.

In short our understanding, whether from a spiritual aspect *or* a scientific one, is still very limited when it comes to the nature of our existence or that of the wider universe (or universes). In coming decades, centuries or, perhaps, millennium some of these mysteries may be further explored and better understood. In the meantime, centuries of practice in diverse religious and spiritual traditions can help us to experience this amazing phenomenon for ourselves and, perhaps, ultimately contribute to that understanding.

Who Can Practice Astral Projection?

The short answer here is "everybody" and that includes you! Neither religious belief (nor lack of it) or any special skills are needed to learn the basic methods of Astral Projection. This book has drawn together simple techniques that have been developed by successful practitioners of Astral Projection which are, in turn drawn from older sources and traditions. This will be the focus of the next and main section of this book, while in the final chapters we'll look at aspects of Astral Projection including the benefits and possible risks.

Chapter 2

Astral Projection; The Basics

In this chapter we'll be taking a look at a number of simple exercises which anyone can practice to achieve Astral Projection and/or an OOBE. Before we do we'll take a look at some of the basic principles and terms that you'll need to understand when applying any of the techniques.

When and How To Practice Astral Projection

Astral Projection is best accomplished when we sleep (though it should not be mistaken with vivid or lucid dreaming) or when we are in a deep state of trance. The latter is not easy to achieve, without years of practice and often with considerable sacrifice. Trance states are often achieved by monks within some traditions, notably the Eastern religions, including Buddhism. However, this method not only takes many years of practice and meditation but requires a level of removal from the everyday world that most of us cannot afford in terms of time, practicality or family life! Practicing Astral Projection during sleep is by far the more accessible method for most of us. Astral Projection can be defined as a state of altered consciousness. In a sense, when we fall asleep, and particularly when we begin to dream, we are entering another form of consciousness. This is the reason that for most people it's the easiest way and the easiest time to practice the art of Astral Projection.

Sleep Paralysis

This is a natural effect that occurs when we sleep. Our brains shut off the signals that are normally sent to our body to respond to the world around us. This is in order to protect us from physical harm when we dream. Our brain interprets the images in dreams as real and does not differentiate between our waking experiences and our sleeping ones. In order to avoid us running, jumping, leaping or making any other physical movement that we might make in response to "external stimuli" the brain simply induces a state of paralysis. Therefore, although we sense movement in our dreams, we don't actually make the movements (or not completely) that are occurring in the dream. Inducing a sleep paralysis state is often used as a technique in Astral Projection for much the same ends. Our experiences are real during Astral Projection and although the technique allows us to travel in the Astral plane and to different parts of the physical world our perceptions can still influence our physical body.

The Hypnagogic State

This is the state that we enter just before sleep, the very border of consciousness and unconscious perception. It is usually the point at which our brains disconnect our physical responses – the sleep paralysis described above. Learning to control this state is essential and it's a technique that can take some practice, although most people will, with time, learn to master it completely.

Relaxation and Meditation

Many people will be familiar with some techniques to achieve both of these ends and they are useful, possibly essential techniques to learn when practicing Astral Projection as the technique requires complete relaxation of the body and the mind. Learning to achieve this state is the first step in learning to Project and without doing so attempts at Astral Projection are likely to have limited results. There are many meditation techniques that you can use to practice relaxation but one of the most effective (and by far the easiest to master) is Mindfulness meditation. This does not require learning to clear the mind but to experience only the moment that you are in – and allowing thoughts to flow freely through your mind.

Vibration

this term relates to a sensation that you will experience as your Astral body begins to make its presence felt. Many experience it as a light tingling sensation throughout the body and you may also experience a feeling that you body is beginning to "float". This is the Astral Body "lifting" from the physical, it is rarely an unpleasant sensation and often you will feel that your body is filled with light and energy.

Astral Projection Techniques

The aim of Astral Projection is to separate the physical body and the Astral, or spirit, body. Many of the techniques involve visualization to enable you to literally "split" the two bodies. The techniques described in this section are based on this principle but offer a number of different ways to achieve this end – some may work for you and some may not. For most individuals different techniques work and it's often a case of practicing several, possibly many, in order to establish what works best for you. Astral Projection is possible for anybody – but it can take time and patience to become proficient. While some people fear that Astral Projection is "dangerous" or may leave you unable to reconnect with your physical body, this is not in fact the case. We'll look at the dangers or risks involved with Astral Projection towards the end of the book.

However, for the time being, it's important to understand that our physical and Astral bodies are intrinsically connected and it is simply not possible to "disconnect" them or to lose your way back to one, or the other! .

Achieving Separation

This is a simple exercise which should enable you to practice separating your physical and Astral bodies. The aim is simply to travel no further than another part of the room in which you are located! Before you begin this exercise choose a point in the room – an object or a feature such as a cabinet or bookshelf, drawers or simply a corner of the room. Examine this area or object carefully, feel any parts of it and try to absorb the "sense" of being in that place.

Now settle yourself in a comfortable position and begin your relaxation. Close your eyes and focus on the darkness, your breathing and allow yourself to enter a hypnagogic state. In this state, begin to visualize the object you have "learned". Focus on this for a few seconds, then on the darkness in front of you, for a further few seconds.

Keep repeating this process until you begin to feel yourself entering a state of vibration. Shortly after entering this state you should achieve full separation of your body.

The Rope

A technique popularized by the mystic, Robert Bruce, this is a simple and often very effective Projection technique. Once you are settled, relaxed and entering the place between waking and sleeping, simply imagine a rope hanging down above you. Keeping your eyes closed and your body relaxed and visualize yourself reaching for the rope. Imagine the feelings of climbing the rope, the way in which your muscles would tense, the weight of your body. Do not tense your muscles for real. Continue to mentally climb, and speed up the process of doing so. Vibrations should develop relatively quickly during the process and continue to speed up the pace of your ascent until separation is achieved.

Exhaust Yourself

Separation of the physical and Astral bodies can be achieved by keeping the mind alert but the body exhausted. During the day be as active as you can. Take a long walk, a run, stay busy and stay up late. Keep your mind active by reading, writing or playing games which require a high level of mental activity – chess is a good example. When you feel that you can no longer stay awake go to bed and relax your body. You will be ready to fall into a deep sleep but, instead, concentrate on the feelings of going to sleep, allowing your body to "fall-away".

You will quickly enter a hypnagogic state and at this point begin to feel and hear the symptoms of vibration. As this develops simply imagine (without really doing it) getting up. Your physical body will fall into sleep and your Astral will rapidly separate.

Falling Awake

This technique can be performed early in the morning or late at night. In the morning, when you first awake simply lie still and relax. Keep your eyes closed and try to force sleep to return. You should quickly enter a vibrational state and at this point force your Astral body to "get up". This can be a rapid technique and very effective but will need practice; the trick is to recognize the Hypnagogic state as it develops and train your Astral Body to "jump" away at this point. At night this should be practiced as you begin to drift off, allow your brain to think you are going to sleep but quickly pull your Astral body away from the physical.

Focus on the Familiar

At the point of deep relaxation, focus on a very familiar, every day object. Something mundane that you handle all of the time, but barely notice with your conscious mind, is an excellent choice. Good examples are house or car keys and, in the modern world, a smart phone! Visualize how the object feels in your hand, the weight texture and general feel of having the object in your hand. Gradually you will find that you are more aware of your visualized or Astral hand than of the physical one. As the visualization deepens you'll find that your whole Astral body is vibrating at a rate at which you can simply slip fully into it and achieve Projection.

Tunnel Vision

Another popular and easy visualization to achieve Projection is to visualize a long, dark tunnel with a distant, white light at the end. Place yourself in this tunnel and imagine yourself flying through it, faster and faster as the visualization proceeds. You will begin to experience the vibrational state. This state normally induce sounds and visions, but these should be ignored, simply focus on the light and continue speeding towards it; as you enter it, your Astral and physical bodies will separate.

The Thirst Technique

This technique was developed by Sylvan Muldoon – an early pioneer in Astral travel and altered states of consciousness. The technique should *only* be practiced by those in good physical health and should not be used frequently. While it is *very* effective, it's not considered good for your health in the longer term! Even those in general good health may wish to avoid using it on a regular basis. Simply avoid drinking any fluids for several hours before you go to sleep. While Muldoon recommended eating salt to increase the sense of thirst – this is far from sensible health wise. However, eating a meal with salty foods several hours before going to bed and avoiding fluids will create a strong thirst. When you are ready to go to bed, place a large glass or pitcher of water in your room. Ensure it's out of easy reach and, as you begin to fall asleep focus. on this water. Imagine how it would feel to reach for it, pour a glass and take a long deep gulp. Do not act, physically, on this but keep the visualization both strong and at the forefront of your mind. As you drift off to sleep the desire for the water and visualization should form a very powerful urge within your body and this will be more than enough to cause separation between your Astral and physical bodies.

Chapter 3

The Realities and Benefits of Astral Projection

While the techniques in the previous chapter will help you to achieve Astral Projection, the next big question is what you can do once you have projected!

The Physical Plane *and* Astral Projection

In reality, in your early attempts at Astral Projection, the most likely place you will visit is the room in which your physical body is situated. Sound boring? You'll be surprised. This experience alone can be both fascinating and unsettling. At first, your abilities will be largely limited to the immediate vicinity of your own body. Don't be put off or disappointed by this. In some senses it's a safety net for both our physical and Astral bodies. Projection takes a considerable amount of energy. This energy is both psychic and can also be physical in that when you awake from Projection you may well feel physically drained.

Take your time to build your strength and begin simply by exploring your own immediate environment. In fact, as you fly quietly around, you'll experience this environment from a very different angle. Be aware that most animals have a sensitivity to the spirit world and some, particularly cats and dogs, will most likely sense your presence. This is particularly true if you have a close bond with them, but unless they are of a nervous nature in normal life, they'll almost certainly be unafraid of your astral presence!

Some individuals are also more sensitive to the spirit, or Astral, body than others and may quickly sense your presence. In addition, those people who have a strong bond with you may also find that they sense your presence on some level, regardless of their normal level of psychic ability. This may be subtle and it may be something that they don't mention but be aware that when you first begin traveling Astrally the experience can be "weird", strange and unsettling for you and for those around you. While it may be pleasant to learn to Astrally visit loved ones and reassure yourself that they are safe and well, it's sometimes more respectful and appropriate to use your physical body to call!

As you develop your skills in Projection you'll be able to move further afield. Travel in the neighborhood, or above it. Developing your skills will be best achieved by visiting places that you know well with your physical body and you'll become stronger both at the technique and in psychic energy. Think of it like a work-out for your Astral body. Simply by practicing regularly, often and visiting places that you know well you know well you will build the capabilities of your

Astral body. As you do so you'll also discover that any sense that your physical body is tired after projecting begins to dispel. As you strengthen the Astral body it will rely on its own strength for energy and Projection. In fact, with time, this new level of spiritual energy will begin to "cross-over" to your physical body and you will return from Astral Projection feeling physically energized.

The Benefits of Astral Projection

Astral Projection can be exciting and terrifying at first! But why would you wish to experience this type of consciousness anyway? In reality we all routinely project to other planes of consciousness as we fall asleep and dream. However, being able to control what we do an where we go, particularly which planes of consciousness we visit when we do is a valuable and rewarding experience.

The Joy of Flying

The first and perhaps most obvious benefit of Projection is simply the joy of being able to fly through the air and see the real, physical world from a whole new perspective. The sky, in this case, is not the limit as there are very few limits at all! You can skim the surface of the oceans, dive deep into their depths or travel beyond the earth to distant planets. The "speed of spirit" is faster than the speed of light and you can, with practice, explore deep into the physical universe.

Life after Death

In an era where religious beliefs and practices are being challenged on a daily basis, Astral Projection techniques can offer many of us a reassuring glimpse of life beyond "death". Physical death is, in reality, simply a change of state, a step in a much longer spiritual journey. Those who become proficient in Astral Projection, will discover the power and comfort that the experience brings as we begin to understand this fully on a deeper level. Our fear of death is often deep-rooted and one that is shared across the globe by all people. Astral Projection will normally remove this fear from both your conscious and unconscious minds. It simply provides reassurance that there is more to life than life itself!

There's More to Life (or Lives)

As your skills develop in Astral Projection you'll begin to experience glimpses, at first, and, eventually, more detailed knowledge or your past lives. This is actually a very important step in our spiritual development. Each time we are born on Earth in physical form we forget these lives, although the lessons in our current lives are the results of experiences and actions in previous ones. Astral Projection is a valuable technique which allows us to reconnect with our true spirit and our broader existence over time. We can more fully understand our own purpose in this life and better address the lessons and challenges we must learn and overcome to create growth and in our spiritual being. Very much depends on how you choose to respond to these lessons but Astral Projection can effectively speed up your spiritual progress and development. This is, in fact, the main reason that it is practiced in many religious traditions, particularly in Buddhism.

Spirit Guidance

We all have spirit guides who watch over us and offer signs in our current lives. Few people connect with these guides in a real sense but doing so can be very valuable. While most people will learn from their spirit guides unknowingly, or receive protection without realizing it, once you are proficient at Astral Projection you will soon meet these guides. This is likely to happen early on in your practice of Astral Projection; the Astral plane is where these guides exist and they will be keen to protect you and offer assistance in this realm. Be open, honest and willing to work with your guides. The real benefit here is that you'll be able to recognize their protection and influence more clearly in your daily, physical life. Most people experience this guidance and protection as simply finding that coincidences or dreams occur in their lives which lead them to make decisions. There is little coincidence about this! Meeting your guides gives you the opportunity to recognize and respond to their influence in the real world, making your path through life much easier.

Expanded Knowledge

Humans have lived on the earth for tens of thousands of years and have learned much during this time. The current pool of knowledge that is available to us in the real, physical world, is only a fraction of the whole that has been gathered during this time. Only that which has been written down or preserved in some way is available to us in the physical world. In the Astral world, all of human knowledge and experience is pooled into a greater consciousness. On the Astral plane you have the opportunity to explore this incredible resource and to learn from both ancient traditions and teachers, as well as beings who have reached a higher level of enlightenment and no longer incarnate in the physical world. Your own spirit guides will offer a starting point in your search for knowledge and can help you access knowledge, learning and teachings that have been long lost to the physical world. Think of it as being a little like access to the Internet – only expanded infinitely!

Psychic Ability

As you become proficient at Projection your sensitivity to your own energy system and the wider energies at work in the universe will become attuned. This inevitably leads to what many describe as psychic ability. You will see the world more clearly (clairvoyance) and you will also develop a greater sense of telepathy and empathy in your dealings with others. You may also begin to experience premonitions and find that telling the future becomes second nature. Be aware that these gifts can be unsettling and be careful of how you use them – especially in relation to other people. Telepathic abilities or premonitions can help you see the future but you should focus on what these can teach you, rather than use them to influence others. Each of us has a path that we must travel and, although it is often tempting to influence the direction that others take, our own path, not that of others, should always be our primary focus.

The Walking, Talking Dead

On the Astral planes you will, almost inevitably, meet relatives and friends who have passed on. This can be a deeply comforting experience and, again, instill a sense of confidence in the fact that there is life beyond death. In general, relatives and ancestors may have a great deal of information and guidance to give. It's important to note that you may well meet relatives from very distant generations and these will be able to offer some deep insight into your own past, your true nature and your path in this life. Don't expect Cleopatra or Mark Anthony – often our distant ancestors turn out to be just as amazing and prosaic as us!

Broader Outlooks

Our experiences in our physical life create knowledge. This is also true of those on the Astral plane. These experiences enrich us as individuals, help us to grow emotionally and intellectually, give us a wider perspective on life and our place in the world and the universe. Self-knowledge is often enhanced by Astral Projection, as is intellectual power and emotional depth. Astral Projection also creates a greater understanding of our spiritual side; many of us are only aware of our physical body and its needs during our life. Understanding and being aware of the Astral body can help to balance these two aspects of the self – creating a rounder, healthier body and soul.

Healing Qualities

Healing is also a crucial aspect that many people find is one of the most important benefits to be gained from practicing

Astral Projection. Healing both the self, others and the wider world can be achieved as we learn to balance our own energy and that which we see around us. This can be physical healing or mental and emotional. Learning to heal others is both a benefit and a joy that will make the practice of Astral Projection worthwhile in itself.

Chapter 4

Astral Projection; The Dangers

In this final chapter we'll take a look at some of the myths and facts surrounding the big question about Astral Projection. How dangerous is it? It may seem odd that we've left this until the last part of this book but, in fact, Astral Projection is not, intrinsically, dangerous.   We've taken the most commonly held fears and questions that people have relating to Projection and hope that the information will be of reassurance.

Can I Die?

One of the first questions on most people's lips is "can I die while projecting?"; the short answer is "yes" and "no" but the issue is even more complex than that. First of all, let's look at the "yes"; any of us can die, at any time and this includes while we are projecting. In reality, this means if your home catches fire in the night, if intruders break in or if an earthquake occurs, then yes, you can physically die from normal causes both natural, accidental or through violence, just as you could in your sleep. The risk that your physical body will not become aware in time of any danger is actually very small. Our Astral and physical bodies operate together at all times, even when we've separated the two states of consciousness are intrinsically linked. The cord that ties them together will remain intact and if physical danger threatens your Astral body will return at a speed that even science cannot imagine. By the same token, your physical body will "call" your Astral body back to itself if any real danger threatens your Astral presence. Astral travel can take place over infinite distances in a split second and the return journey is just as instant.

In terms of the "no" part of this answer, we're really talking about whether you can be killed on the Astral Plane by other beings present in that plane. Some argue that if this was possible, then we would not know, as the individual would not be here to tell us. However, they would be there (on the Astral plane) to tell us and it's not a subject that comes up! In fact, the cord that ties us to our physical body must be cut for us to die in the physical plane. This cord is strong and it will not, cannot, be cut by psychic means. In addition, if you find yourself in difficult situations on the Astral plane you can easily call up protective forces from ascended masters (including Christ) and your own spirit guides. This help and protection will always be forthcoming and offered without fear, favor or judgment. It is *never* withheld and if you ever feel real fear on the Astral Plane, simply focus on the concept of requiring help, visualize white, healing light and move towards it.

Demonic Possession

This is a major fear amongst many people. "Demons" will be encountered at some point in your journey. They are negative energies, often souls who have become trapped in the Astral Plane and have not yet progressed far enough spiritually to be re-born and continue their journey. They are particularly keen to find ways back to the physical plane and may see you as a short-cut! However, protecting yourself against them is simple. Again, call on spirits to help you angels, masters or ascended souls (those who no longer incarnate on Earth). Your spirit guides will also readily come to your aid. Also, again, simply envisage being in a lighter, whiter place, and you will move away towards it effortlessly. Help and protection will always be at hand. In terms of possession, no negative entity can take control of your spirit or your physical body, without your permission. Some may try to trick or persuade you into this but, again, simply call for help and assistance from more powerful and ascended beings. If, as you prepare to enter your physical body again, you encounter less-pleasant entities trying to block you or waiting in the room where your physical body lies, simply tell them to leave. Many people find it hard to believe that this is as simple as it seems; however, "demons" are simply spirits who are not yet ready to re-incarnate, or entities that cannot do so. There place is not the physical world, it is yours. Explain this to them and re-iterate it is time for them to leave. They may seem unwilling, but they cannot argue with this fact!

Lost or Strayed

Some people fear that once they leave their body they may get lost and not be able to find their way back to it. This will not happen. You may be delayed on your journey but the best analogy that can be applied is to imagine you were traveling abroad. You may not get back when, or in quite the way you had planned, however, when you return to your own country you will always be able to find your own home. The link between your spiritual and physical body is simply too strong to break or to lose. As with the issues above, call on spirit guides or ascended souls to guide you back to your home and your body. Any delay will be short and you will find that as you practice Projection more often, delays become a thing of the past.

Conclusion

Thank you again for reading this book!

I hope this book was able to help you to understand the basic methods of achieving Astral Projection and the principles behind the technique. Astral Projection has many amazing benefits and is a subject on which you will find there is much more to learn. I hope that you have found this book useful in providing you with all the basic information that you need to begin your journey with Astral Projection.

The next step is to begin employing some of the techniques described in the book and exploring the world, and then the universe (or universes) around you! The very best of luck!

Finally, if you enjoyed this book, please take the time to share your thoughts and post a review on Amazon. It'd be greatly appreciated!

Thank you and good luck!

About the Author

I want to thank you for giving me the opportunity to spend some time with you!

For the last 10 years of my life I have studied, practiced and shared my love of spirituality and internal development. I kept diaries for years documenting the incredible changes that graced my life. This passion for writing has blossomed into a new chapter in my life where publishing books has become a full time career.

I feel extremely blessed and fortunate to have the opportunity to share my message with you! Each of my books are written to inspire others to explore the many aspects of their internal world. My goal is to touch the lives of others in a positive way and hopefully be the catalyst of positive change in this world :)

I am forever grateful for your support and I know you will get immense value through my books. I am really looking forward to serve you and give you great insight into my passions!

Your Friend

Mia Rose

CPSIA information can be obtained
at www.ICGtesting.com
Printed in the USA
LVHW041737081020
668326LV00014B/1567